# NATIVE AMERICAN
# MYTHS

## Neil Morris

Skyview
Books

an imprint of

WINDMILL
BOOKS

New York

Published in 2009 by Windmill Books, LLC
303 Park Avenue South, Suite # 1280, New York, NY 10010-3657

Copyright © 2009 by Arcturus Publishing Ltd.

Series concept: Alex Woolf
Editor: Alex Woolf
Illustrators: Fiona Sansom and Graham Kennedy
Designer: Ian Winton

Publisher Cataloging Data

Morris, Neil, 1946–
        Native American myths / Neil Morris ; [illustrators, Fiona Sansom and
Graham Kennedy].
                p.        cm. – (Myths from many lands)
        Includes bibliographical references and index.
        Summary: This book provides a brief introduction to early Native American
civilization, a retelling of fifteen Native American myths, and a who's who of characters.
ISBN 978-1-60754-227-8 (library edition)
ISBN 978-1-60754-228-5 (paperback)
ISBN 978-1-60754-229-2 (6-pack)
        Indian mythology—North America—Juvenile literature    2. Tales—North
America    3. Legends—North America    [1. Indians of North America—Folklore]
I. Sansom, Fiona    II. Kennedy, Graham    III. Title    IV. Series
        398.2/097—dc22

Printed in the United States

# CONTENTS

# INTRODUCTION

**M**any thousands of years ago, hunters in search of food crossed a narrow land bridge from their Asian homeland to North America. Today, this strait between Russia and Alaska is covered by sea. These ancestors of Native Americans were the first people to reach America. Groups of them moved south. They crossed mountain ranges and rivers to reach vast plains, forests, and deserts.

## DIFFERENT TRADITIONS

Wherever they went, Native Americans adapted to their surroundings. They learned skills and formed traditions that suited the places they lived. They also helped each other. Families joined together and formed bands and larger groups called tribes. Within each tribe, everyone spoke the same language.

ARCTIC

ARCTIC

NORTH-
WEST
COAST

SUBARCTIC
FOREST

GREAT
PLATEAU

GREAT
PLAINS

GREAT
BASIN

CALIFORNIA

SOUTHWEST
PUEBLO
REGION

NORTHEAST
WOODLANDS

SOUTHEAST
WOODLANDS

N
W
E
S

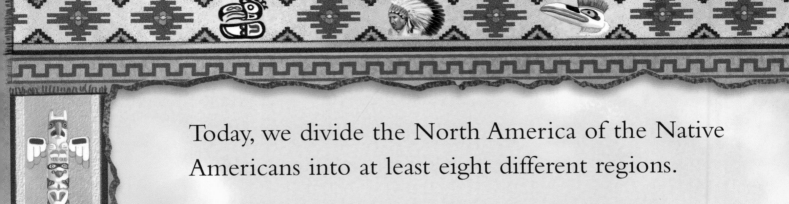

Today, we divide the North America of the Native Americans into at least eight different regions.

## MYTHS AND STORIES

People's beliefs and myths varied in different places, because they were based on their personal experiences. Hunting tribes told stories of animal spirits. Farmers spoke of spirits who controlled the land, rain and crops.

Coastal people were more interested in sea spirits. Myths about the creation of the world were similar across the continent. Some myths were linked to special religious ceremonies, while others were told purely to entertain listeners, especially children. Many were stories of brave heroes, whose lives and actions could inspire everyone.

## TRIBES AND CULTURES

There are myths from different tribes and from all the cultural regions, in this book. They include: the

Hopi tribe of the southwest Pueblo region; the Micmac of the northeast woodlands; the Inuit of the Arctic; the Tlingit of the northwest coast; the Cherokee of the southeast woodlands; the Omaha of the Great Plains; the Ojibwa of the subarctic forest; and the Ute of the Great Basin.

Native American myths were passed on down the generations, as older people told the stories to youngsters. Most were not written down. Some may have been forgotten, and others have changed over the years. The myths that remain still delight listeners and readers today.

# IN THE BEGINNING

At the very beginning of time, there was nothing but endless space. Then Tawa, the sun god, created the first world. It was a pitch-black place, deep beneath the earth. Next Tawa created people to live in this dark, underground world.

As time passed, the people had children, and soon there were so many that they were pushing each other for space. When Tawa saw that the people were quarrelling, he sent a messenger to the first world.

The sun god's messenger was called Spider Woman. She told the people that the first world would soon be destroyed by fire. They must leave quickly.

She planted a reed and told the people to use it as a ladder. They did so at once, climbing up the reed and clambering through a hole into the second world. They discovered that this was also an underground cave, and before long it was just as crowded as the first world was before.

So, Spider Woman once again led the people up the reed ladder, through a hole, into a third world. This time they pulled the ladder up before everyone could join them.

When they saw that the new world was also underground, the people were disappointed. But then Tawa gave them fire, so that they could make torches to light their way.

Before long the people started arguing again. The men blamed the women for the quarrels, and the women blamed the men. It was time for Spider Woman to plant a new reed. She told the people they must leave at once, because floods would soon destroy their world.

When the men and women climbed up through the hole, they stood on the ground of the fourth world. This one had its own light, and when the people looked up, instead of a rocky roof they saw an enormous blue sky. They were happy in the fourth world, the one that we call earth.

# GLUSKAP AND THE OWL'S FEATHER

Gluskap and his brother Malsum helped create the world. Gluskap made plants for people to eat, but Malsum had an evil streak. He made poisonous plants.

One day, Malsum told his brother proudly, "All that can harm me is a fern's root. Can anything harm you?"

"Just one thing," Gluskap replied. "An owl's feather." As soon as he heard these words, Malsum rushed off with his bow and shot an owl. Taking one of the bird's feathers, he crept up behind his brother. When the feather touched Gluskap, he fell to the ground. Malsum ran off in triumph.

But Gluskap had tricked his brother. The owl's feather did him no harm. Gluskap dug up a fern, cut off its root, crept up on his brother and touched him with it. Malsum fell down dead.

Gluskap felt sorry for his brother and soon brought him back to life. But to teach him a lesson, he turned him into a big grey wolf.

13

# RAVEN AND THE MOON

**O**ne day, Raven overheard an old fisherman talking to his daughter about a box of light. Now Raven was a trickster, and he loved shiny things. So he turned himself into a baby boy and spirited his way into the old man's house. The daughter was delighted when she found the baby.

When the baby started crying, the woman gave him toys to play with, but the baby pushed them away. One day the fisherman brought out a beautifully carved box.

The baby grabbed the box from the man and opened it. Inside he found a smaller box, and inside that another, and then another.

When at last the baby opened the tenth box, he saw a bright round ball. He turned straight back into Raven, took the ball in his beak and flew out of the smoke hole. Then Raven flew up high and threw the ball into the sky. And there it remains to this day. We call it the Moon.

# SPIRIT OF THE SEA

**S**edna was a beautiful girl who lived with her father in the frozen north. One day a young man asked to marry her. Her father told her, firmly, to accept the offer and she obeyed.

Then the man took Sedna away to a rocky island. Suddenly a change came over him and he showed himself for what he really was — a seabird!

Some weeks later, Sedna's father came to visit and she begged him to take her home. On their way, the seabird dived from the sky and attacked their kayak. Sedna fell into the freezing ocean. When she tried to save herself, her father was so frightened of the seabird's attacks that he chopped off Sedna's fingers. They turned into seals and swam away. Sedna clung on, but the old man cut off her hands, which turned into whales.

Then Sedna sank beneath the waves, where she became the Spirit of the Sea. She lives there still, ruling over seals, whales and all the other sea animals.

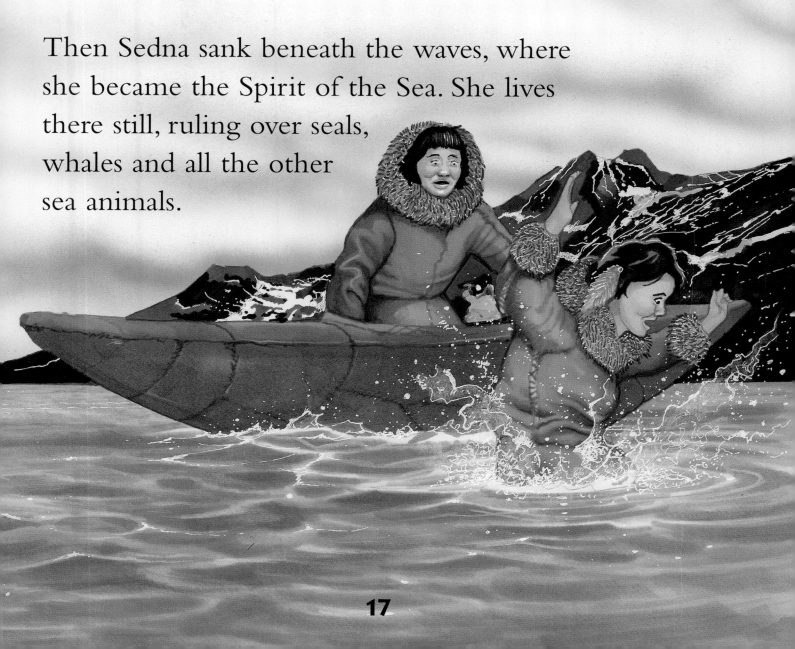

# RABBIT CATCHES THE SUN

**E**very morning, Rabbit left his tepee (tent) to go hunting with his bow and arrows. But he never caught anything, because someone else always seemed to beat him to it and frighten all the animals away. So Rabbit got up earlier and earlier. But even at the crack of dawn, he was still too late.

Rabbit decided to catch his rival and teach him a lesson. So one night he crept out and set a trap made of one of his bowstrings.

The next morning, Rabbit got up so early

that it was still dark. He rushed off to his trap and was astonished to find that he had caught a big, bright, fiery ball. "Let me go at once!" roared the Sun.

The frightened Rabbit quickly cut the bowstring, and the Sun soared up into the sky. But Rabbit had got so close that some of his fur was scorched, and you can still see the mark on him today.

# THE BRINGER OF CORN

Long ago, an old woman lived with her grandson. When the boy was seven, she made him a bow and arrows and sent him out hunting, but the boy returned empty-handed.

"What has a bushy tail and runs up trees?" he asked. "A squirrel," Grandmother replied. "Shoot it and bring it home to eat."

The next day the boy did as was told, and Grandmother made him a dinner of meat and corn. "And what flies from tree to tree?" the boy asked. "A bird," said Grandmother. "Shoot it and bring it home to eat."

The next day the boy asked, "What is big with round ears and no tail?" "A bear," said Grandmother. "Shoot it and bring it home to eat."

But the boy always wondered where the corn came from, so he followed Grandmother into the storehouse. Peeping inside, he saw her scratch her legs until corn poured into her basket. His grandmother was the bringer of corn.

# THE STRONGEST MAN

A chief had four sons. The three oldest were brave and hard-working, but the youngest son, Duktuthl, seemed weak and lazy. All anyone saw him do was lie by the fire all day. But before dawn, Duktuthl always went out into the woods to practice hunting and get fit. By the time the others got up, he was dozing by the fire again.

One summer, the chief's village was challenged to a wrestling match by another tribe. The opponents brought with them a giant of a man, who quickly defeated the chief's three oldest sons.

Then Duktuthl stepped forward. When the giant rushed at him, he grabbed him by the arm and flung him into the air. The giant landed with a terrible thump, and did not get up.

From then on, the chief, his sons and the villagers never disturbed Duktuthl when he lay by the fire. One day, some strangers arrived and asked Duktuthl to visit their chief.

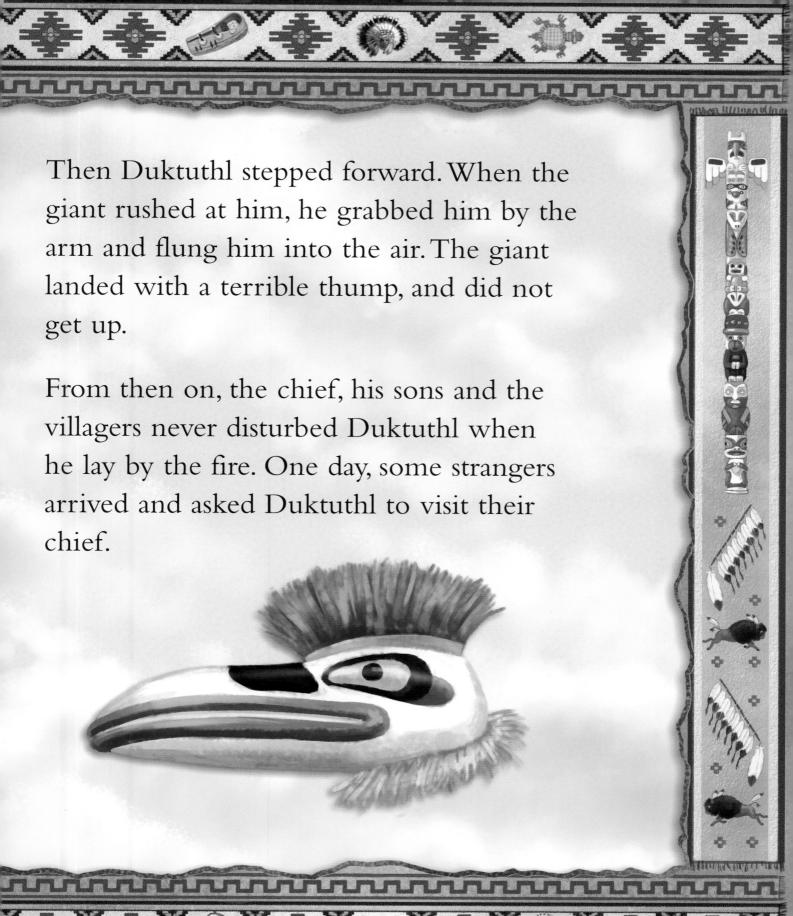

Duktuthl jumped into the strangers' canoe, but once they were at sea, a whirlpool opened up and sucked them to the bottom of the ocean. There Duktuthl saw an old man with a long pole on his chest. "I am very old and sick," the chief said. "Now you must take over."

So Duktuthl lay down and placed the pole on his chest. On top of the pole was the world, and Duktuthl has been holding it up ever since.

# OTTER HEART

**A** boy named Otter Heart lived with his sister in the middle of a great forest. Their parents were dead, so the children lived alone. One day Otter Heart asked his sister to make ten pairs of moccasins. Then he set off into the forest in search of other people.

As he went, he hung the moccasins from branches, so that he could find his way back. Many days later, he reached a village. Otter Heart spent some time with the villagers before using the moccasins to guide him home. The lonely days were over for Otter Heart and his sister.

# SEVEN STAR SISTERS

One evening a young man went fishing in a lake near his village. He was just putting his canoe in the water when he heard singing. Then he saw a basket come down from the sky and land on the far shore.

The young man watched from behind a tree as seven beautiful girls jumped out of the basket. The girls joined hands and danced on the shore as they sang.

The young man was so entranced that he started singing too. Startled, the girls ran back to the basket and were gone in seconds.

When the young man went back to the lake the next evening, to his delight, the same thing happened. This time, while the girls danced and sang, the young man crept closer. Then he quickly grabbed one of the girls by the arm, as the others ran for the basket and were gone.

"Let me go at once!" the girl cried.

"I will, but first please tell me who you are," the young man said.

"We are daughters of the Sun and Moon," the girl replied. 'At night we are stars in the sky, and that is where we belong."

"When your sisters return, I will come to the sky with you," the young man said.

The next evening the other girls returned, and their sister persuaded them to let the young man into their basket. But when they reached the sky, the Sun was very angry. He told his daughters off for visiting earth and demanded to know what the young man wanted.

"I love your daughter," the young man said. "and I ask your permission to marry her." The seventh daughter blushed and smiled, and the Sun said he would allow the marriage if she wished it. She nodded, and the young man joined the sisters as they took their places in the sky. The Seven Sisters, which we call the Pleiades, are there to this day.

# COYOTE FINDS FIRE

**O**ne day, when Coyote was out hunting, he came across a burned reed. This made him think. No one in his village had ever seen fire, but Coyote was clever enough to know that it existed. That very day he set out west, in search of fire.

Some days later, Coyote reached a tall, black mountain. At the top he saw a group of people dancing around some flickering flames. "That's it," he thought, "fire!"

Coyote greeted the Fire People as a friend, and they invited him to join their dance. Coyote made himself a headdress of dried reeds and hopped around the fire with his hosts.

Then, suddenly, he threw his headdress into the flames. It caught fire at once, and Coyote grabbed it, tied it to his tail and ran off at top speed. When he reached home, Coyote lit some twigs with the embers on his tail. And soon all the surrounding villages had the knowledge of fire.

# FEATHER WOMAN AND MORNING STAR

**A** young girl named Feather Woman loved watching the morning star as it rose in the sky before dawn. One day she left her prairie camp to collect firewood. She had not gone far when she met a handsome young man.

"Do you not know me?" the stranger asked. "I am Morning Star. I saw you watching me in the sky and fell in love with you. Will you come home with me to the land of Star People?"

When Feather Woman agreed, Morning Star placed a bush full of silken threads on

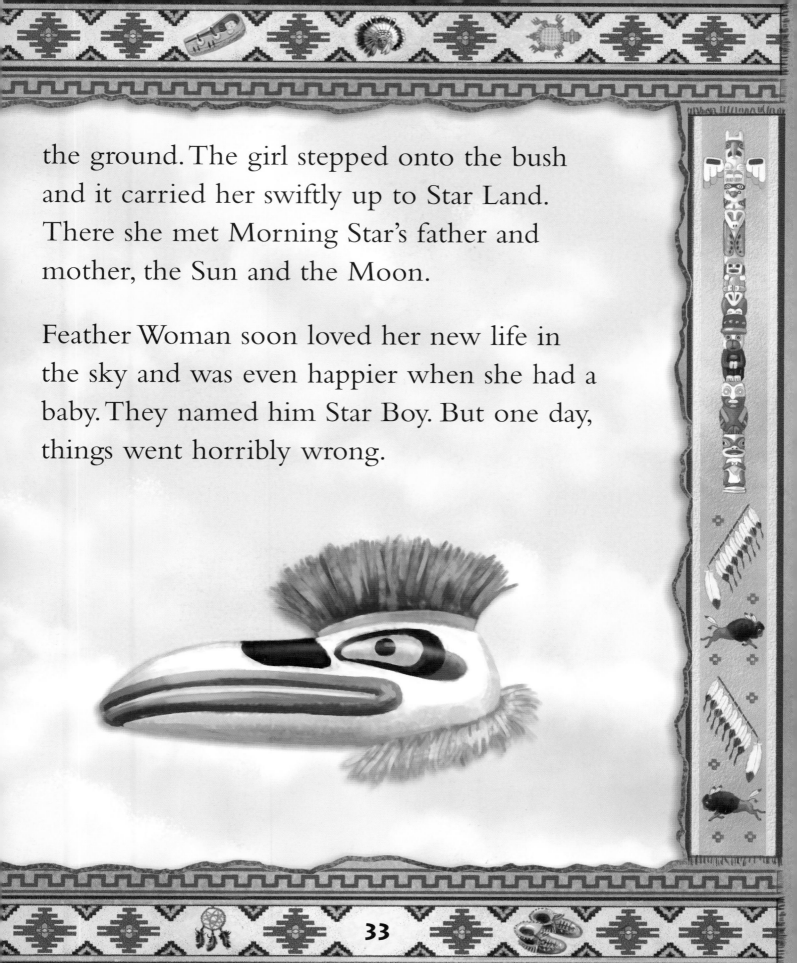

the ground. The girl stepped onto the bush and it carried her swiftly up to Star Land. There she met Morning Star's father and mother, the Sun and the Moon.

Feather Woman soon loved her new life in the sky and was even happier when she had a baby. They named him Star Boy. But one day, things went horribly wrong.

Feather Woman was out gathering roots and berries when she came across a giant turnip. Before she could touch it, the Moon warned her off, saying the turnip was sacred to Star People.

Later, two white cranes swooped down and started digging up the turnip with their beaks. Feather Woman helped with her digging stick, and at last the turnip came out of the ground, leaving a huge hole.

Through the gaping hole in the sky, Feather Woman could see the prairies of her old home on earth. She was just about to put the turnip back when she heard the Sun's booming voice. "Disobedient girl!" he roared. "Since you like to look at the earth, you had better go back there at once!"

Morning Star pleaded with his father, but it was no good. Feather Woman was sent back to earth with her baby, never to return. Once again, all she could do was watch the morning star rise in the sky before dawn.

# SCAR FACE

Star Boy was left alone when his mother, Feather Woman, died of a broken heart. Still he grew brave and strong, but with one unusual feature. The young man had a large mark on his cheek, and the other boys called him Scar Face.

One day, Scar Face walked to the edge of the prairie and saw a golden path leading up to the sky. Climbing the path, he was startled to see a man being attacked by seven cranes.

Scar Face quickly ran at the birds, striking them with his club and frightening them off. The grateful man looked closely at Scar Face and recognized his son. "I am Morning Star, your father," the man said. "Welcome!"

Morning Star's father, the Sun, was so pleased with Scar Face that he taught the young man the secrets of the sun dance. "Take this knowledge to your tribe on earth," he said, "and it will bring them health and happiness." And that is what Scar Face did.

# LITTLE DEER

**L**ong ago, when humans discovered the bow and arrow, they started hunting too many animals. They even killed those they did not need for food or clothing. The animals met to discuss this problem.

The bears were angry and wanted to fight back and kill the humans. Other animals disagreed but had no idea what to do.

Then Little Deer spoke up. "Humans will always hunt animals," he said. "But they must show respect and hunt only when they need to. Otherwise, they will kill us all. First, they must hold a ceremony to ask permission to hunt. Then they must ask forgiveness of any animal they kill and respect its spirit."

All the animals agreed with Little Deer's wise words. So that very night he crept up to sleeping hunters and whispered in their ears, telling them what they must do. The next morning, the hunters thought they had been dreaming. And from then on they followed the new hunting rules.

# TRICKING THE FLYING FACE

**T**he Flying Faces were horrible bodiless heads that destroyed everything and ate human flesh. Everyone was frightened of them – everyone, that is, except a brave young woman in one woodland village.

She said she would never run away from such monsters.

One night the young woman heard strange noises: swishing hair, snapping teeth and a sniffing nose. She knew a Flying Face had come into her longhouse and was right behind her.

Everyone else had run away, but the brave young woman stayed calm. She took a forked stick, picked up a red-hot stone from the fire and pretended to eat it. "Mmmm, delicious," she said, licking her lips near the stone.

The woman's trick worked. The greedy Flying Face opened its jaws and gulped a mouthful of red-hot stones from the fire. There was a moment's silence before the Face screamed in agony and shot out through the door. And no Flying Face was ever seen in that village again.

# FLYING TURTLE

**O**ne autumn, Turtle saw flocks of birds getting ready for a journey. "Where are you off to?" he asked.

"We're flying south for the winter," a bird replied. "Brrrrr, it's getting cold here. We're off!"

"May I come too?" asked Turtle. "I know I can't fly, but there must be a way."

The bird laughed and laughed, but then she had an idea. If Turtle could hold onto a stick with his mouth, some birds could grab the stick with their claws and carry him along.

Turtle thought this was an excellent idea, and they set off.

All went well until Turtle decided to ask where they were. When he opened his mouth to speak, he let go of the stick and fell to the ground with a thump. Then poor Turtle crawled into the nearest pond, burrowed into the mud and went to sleep for the winter. And turtles have hibernated ever since. It's less painful than flying.

# WHO'S WHO IN NATIVE AMERICAN MYTHS

## COYOTE

The wolf-like Coyote is a trickster who usually causes trouble. He is sometimes the younger brother of another animal, such as Wolf, Puma or Eagle. In our story, Coyote helps others.

## FLYING FACES

Among the Iroquois tribes, these were evil demons. Humans who made masks of the demons, called False Faces, could cure people of illness.

## GLUSKAP

In the northeastern woodlands, Gluskap was a great hero. He came to the shores of the world in a stone canoe, which turned into an island. Gluskap created all the good things in the world, including the earth, the air, the animals and the people.

## MALSUM

According to Algonquin myth, Gluskap's brother Malsum was evil, selfish and destructive. While Gluskap made useful things, Malsum made all the things that were troublesome to humans, such as poisonous plants and snakes.

## RABBIT

Rabbit (or sometimes Hare) is a bold and cunning animal, who lost most of his long, bushy tail in a fight with Bear.

## RAVEN

A member of the crow family, this bird is a trickster. Some peoples of the Arctic also thought of Raven as a creator of the world.

## SCAR FACE

Scar Face, the son of Morning Star, is called Poia by the Blackfoot tribe. He teaches people the wisdom that he learned from the Sun, especially the sun dance, which helps to heal the sick.

## SEDNA

This important Inuit goddess is the spirit of the sea, who rules the ocean depths. She is the goddess of marine animals, especially mammals such as seals and whales.

## SPIDER WOMAN

Among the southwestern tribes, such as the Hopi, Spider Woman is a grandmother who takes the form of a spider. She serves as a messenger for the sun god Tawa.

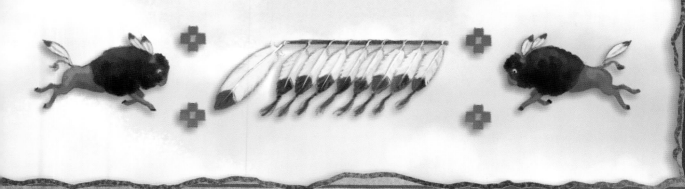

# GLOSSARY

**corn**  A cereal crop, also called maize.

**coyote**  A North American mammal similar to but smaller than the wolf.

**crane**  A long-necked bird.

**embers**  The glowing remains of a fire.

**fern**  A green plant with roots and stems but no flowers.

**hibernate**  Sleep through the winter.

**kayak**  A light canoe made of wood and animal skins.

**longhouse**  A large wooden house occupied by several families.

**moccasin**  A shoe made of soft hide.

**morning star**  Not really a star, but the planet Venus.

**myth**  A traditional story about gods, goddesses, spirits and heroes that often explains how things came about.

**Pleiades**  A cluster of seven stars in the constellation Taurus the Bull.

**prairie**  A grassy plain.

**prehistoric**  In the time before people made written records.

**smoke hole**  An opening in the roof of a tent or house to let out smoke from the fire.

**strait**  A narrow strip of water.

**sun dance**  A ceremony in honor of the sun.

**tepee**  A cone-shaped skin tent on a framework of wooden poles.

**tribe**  A large group of families with the same language, customs and beliefs.

**trickster**  Someone who likes playing tricks on others.

# FURTHER INFORMATION

## BOOKS

Burland, Cottie, and Marion Wood. *North American Indian Mythology*. Chancellor Press, 1996.

Dixon-Kennedy, Mike. *Native American Myth and Legend: An A–Z of People and Places*. Blandford, 1996.

Spence, Lewis. *Native American Myths*. Dover Publications, 2005.

## WEB SITES

To ensure the currency and safety of recommended Internet links, Windmill maintains and updates an online list of sites related to the subject of this book. To access this list of Web sites, please go to www.windmillbks.com/weblinks and select this book's title.

# INDEX

**For more great fiction and nonfiction, go to windmillbks.com.**